NOTHING GOOD WILL GET AWAY

poems by

Chelsea Dodds

Finishing Line Press
Georgetown, Kentucky

NOTHING GOOD WILL GET AWAY

*To anyone searching for the courage
to tell someone how you feel.*

*And to all those who have already found
that courage.*

ACKNOWLEDGMENTS

"Salinas" was originally published in *Poetry Super Highway*
"WYKYK" was originally published in *Raising the Fifth*
"Same Frequency" and "Perception" were originally published in *Roi Fainéant*

Publisher: Leah Huete de Maines
Editor: Christen Kincaid
Cover Art: Chelsea Dodds
Author Photo: Joanna Douglas
Cover Design: Elizabeth Maines McCleavy

Order online: www.finishinglinepress.com
also available on amazon.com

Author inquiries and mail orders:
Finishing Line Press
PO Box 1626
Georgetown, Kentucky 40324
USA

Contents

Dream Boy 1

Koi No Yokan 3

Closer 4

On Raquette Lake 6

Insomnia 7

Manifestation 8

Vibes 9

Reunited 11

Salinas 12

At Point Lobos 14

The Eve of Everything 15

Same Frequency 16

WYKYK 18

In Which I Think We Can Read Each Other's Minds 19

Perception 20

Dream Life 22

Standards 23

My Mother Reads My Tarot Cards 25

Robot Poem 26

The Voice in My Head 27

Release 28

The Next Time Someone Tells Me to Get Over It 29

222 31

Spring Again 32

Dream Boy

I kill off the love interest.
Car crash, the night before
he'll ask out the protagonist.
All the clichés, because I'm 13

and this sounds like
what would happen in a movie.
The love interest is a drummer:
tall, with dark hair and blue eyes,

the comedic relief of the crew
who keeps his true feelings inside.
The protagonist is who I hope to be
when I'm older, bold and unafraid.

As I grow up, I imagine
who the protagonist might date
if the dream boy is dead.
Perhaps the boy's older brother,

or her best friend since kindergarten.
But something feels amiss,
in the story and real life.
The protagonist and love interest

wrote songs over the phone,
embarked on spontaneous adventures
involving skateboards and ice cream,
inside jokes and incessant laughter.

My real-life boyfriend and I
attend concerts with our arms crossed,
barely talking in between sets.
We don't see eye-to-eye.

I worry I've jinxed myself,
that I'll never date the right man
because I killed the fictional version
of my dream person, and therefore

he can't exist in real life, right?

Koi No Yokan

I don't question it at first—

how I'm more interested in talking to you
    than the other teachers at the retreat.

how you share your passion for ceramics and I'm reminded
    of my grandparents who owned a ceramics business.

how we laugh that the group drumming class was too easy,
    and then you say you took lessons as a kid.

how we make each other laugh
    more than anyone else here.

how we always seem to be standing together in group photos,
    always gravitating towards each other.

how you sit next to me on the boat ride back to camp
    and tell me your favorite lines from *Of Mice and Men*.

how you suggest we travel together to Steinbeck's house
    when we've only known each other a few days.

how it feels like I've known you for much longer,
    like we can talk about anything, for hours.

how I know this trip needs to happen,
    even though I have a boyfriend at home I don't know
    how to leave.

how it seems crazy to think of pursuing anything with you,
    but now I can't think about anything or anyone else.

Closer

I've always wished I could swim,
that I could explore open waters
without fear of falling
below the surface,
my nostrils panic-filling
with water as I struggle
to breathe.

I almost drowned as a child,
and sometimes still wake
from nightmares where I'm trapped
under water.
At camp, I watch
as everyone else kayaks
and paddleboards,

a confident balancing act.
They ask if I want to join,
and I decline, not trusting
my body to know
what to do if I tip over.
So when you ask me
to go canoeing with you,

I surprise myself when I agree.
Something about your presence
makes me less afraid.
Maybe it's your calm
baritone voice, the feeling of home
that hugs me like a blanket
whenever you're near.

I'm nervous as we approach
the lake but you reassure me:
the water is only four feet deep,
we won't tip over, but if we do,

we'll be able to stand up.
And besides, we have life jackets
and you've paddled a canoe

plenty of times before.
The water is calm
but closer than I'm used to.
You hold my hand as I step
into the boat bobbing against the dock,
your benevolent blue eyes
glistening in the afternoon sun.

Once we push off,
my nerves die down,
shoulders relax,
and I want to stay
here all day with you.

On Raquette Lake

balancing on uneven rocks
by the bonfire is worth the discomfort
to talk with you a little longer.

the air is thick but the fire detracts mosquitoes
that buzz around lake water, slapping the dock,
preventing any dead air in the conversation.

we compare the college radio shows we each hosted,
reminisce about our favorite 90s computer games,
eventually breaking away from the rest of the group.

we're caught up in our own stories, in predicting
from how far away we can see heat lightning,
in giggles and fist bumps and passing pieces of chocolate

to each other while everyone else makes s'mores.
for a moment, i picture we are somewhere else
in our real lives, and you are my boyfriend

and i feel a sense of peace i have never felt
back home. but then, someone across the fire asks
about my boyfriend, and you go quiet

like we've been caught, like they can read
the desire for a different life on my face,
and i know nothing can ever be the same.

Insomnia

two a.m. back at home
the glare from your phone
keeping you from sleep
as you open and close the same app
and see the green dot
signaling he's also online
and you wonder what he's watching
if he's also searching
for the green dot on your avatar
like Gatsby looked for Daisy's light
and you reread the last messages
you sent each other trying to parse
out any hidden feelings that neither
can vocalize because of relationships
and distance and you want to start up
a new conversation in a way that won't
be weird because clearly neither of you can sleep
but you have nothing of substance to say
and put the phone away.

Manifestation

In my 20s, I write a novel
in which the love interest is a Virgo,
has blue eyes, no tattoos, and drives a Jeep.
I think I wanted the love interest to
have a birthday when the weather is nice.
I think nothing else of it. A decade passes

and I find myself
in a situation similar to my protagonist:
far from home, crushing
on a blue-eyed, Jeep-driving, tattooless Virgo,
unsure if I'll see him again.
I go home and question everything.

The Virgo and I apply together for a grant.
I tell my cousin, who Googles
the compatibility of our signs.
"Virgo and Capricorn are a power couple,"
she squeals. It makes sense.
She says I manifested all of this

by writing the novel.
I'm not sure I agree, but
in the book the protagonist asks
the love interest to join him on a road trip,
the destination the same as the grant location,
and I want to believe.

Vibes

You ask, "Wouldn't it be nice to just be an artist?"
I *heart* the message but I want to say
it's the most attractive thing anyone has ever asked me.

You say, "let's make a joint Instagram page."
You respond, "aww" to a picture of us
in the canoe last summer.

You say, "let's go to England in five years when we can apply for
this grant again."
I say, "let's spend the whole summer there for our 40th birthdays."
You say, "I'm in."
I don't ask if your girlfriend is still around.

You say, "I can't wait to twin in our matching shirts."
You say, "it's like this partnership was meant to be."

We send texts and DMs at late hours,
discussing jobs we worked as teenagers,
field trips we've chaperoned,
King of the Hill episodes.

You send a "sweet dreams" text.
I don't know how to respond.

You send me a video from a race
you're watching with your mom
when I've just woken up
and I'm bummed I'm not there with you both.

We send each other memes about words
and hikes and random things we'll both
find funny. You get my sense of humor
more than anyone else and I don't know how
to tell you that without making it weird.

So I play along,
here for the flattery and support
counting down the weeks until
we see each other again
and hope when we reunite
these feelings will last.

Reunited

For all the anticipation of the last year I'm surprised how calm I am when I actually see you again, outside the airport gate at SFO with a wave and a smile and we greet each other with a hug like we've known each other our whole lives. We unintentionally match in all black and North Face jackets, ease naturally into conversations about when I got glasses and your insecurities about cooking. When we go out for pizza, you coach me through parallel parking despite me saying I'll just pick a different spot, like the summer before when you taught me how to bridge my cards while shuffling. You show me a photo of the girl you broke up with last week and I try to hide my excitement. It's a tranquil excitement, no butterflies in my stomach, just knowing this is where I should be right now. The next day, we eat burritos on a park bench by the water in Oakland, watching dog walkers and talking about Gorillaz, and I know that wherever I am with you is where I feel safest.

Salinas

You turn on the hazard lights and park
halfway through the underpass,
giddy at how the California sun
illuminates your favorite mural in town and
we need to take a picture in front of it now.
Back on the road, we sing along
to Tame Impala while you text your ex
and point out funny license plates
I could maybe text my ex
if we were on better terms.

At lunch, you let me try your horchata.
I hold the cup to my lips and wait
to sip while you excitedly describe
that it tastes like the smell inside Pottery Barn,
and then we both laugh at the accuracy.
When our food arrives, we scoop grilled
cactus onto our plates and you can't
stop smiling over everything new to you
on this trip and I can't stop admiring how
you always find joy in the little things.

"Salinas is a vibe," some friends say
before we travel out there, but I know
our adventures are different,
how we have no interest in the wineries
but we pluck grapes from roadside vineyards
and rush to wash down the sour taste.
How we search quaint neighborhoods
for estate sales we never find. How you park
in the street again to free a piece of prickly pear
and mail it home to New York, and I think
I could drive around aimlessly with you forever.

And in the evenings, when we retire
to the Best Western next to the McDonalds,
in separate but adjacent rooms,

I lie in my bed and listen through the wall
for signs you're awake: a snippet
of phone conversation, the TV, but all
I hear is the hum of the AC and I wonder
if this is the closest I'll ever get to falling
asleep next to you, always divided by walls
and state lines and past lovers who still hold
space in our hearts.

At Point Lobos

we walk along paths abutting steep drop offs,
watching beachgoers and surfers down below
and bonding over our disdain for beach days,
people who spend all their vacations at Disney,
coffee drinkers, running, and religion.

we take no pictures of ourselves—
just the harbor seals, the black birds mistaken
for penguins from afar, the fog hanging low
over the fauna, obscuring the ocean's breadth.
i already know when i look back on this moment

i will remember it as one when nothing else
mattered besides being here with you.
when we take a shortcut to the car,
you hold my hand as i squeeze through
the barbed wire fence, and i don't want to leave.

The Eve of Everything

In Big Sur
we share an apple
that you break in half
with your bare hands.
You suck in your breath
as you grip each side
of the core and pull,
your cheeks turning rosier
than normal.
We walk down the trail
as we snack on the sweet fruit
and laugh at your feat.
We should have videotaped it.
This will never happen again,
unlike the tree limbs larger
than you that you effortlessly
cleared from the trail last summer
at camp, how I was impressed
by your strength but over the past year
have been impressed by so much more.
How you notice little details other people
ignore, how you dream big and follow
your passions and it's inspiring
to be around you. And I worry
telling you how I feel will ruin
everything, like breaking the apple
with your bare hands was a curse,
because why wouldn't it be?
Like it keeps us forever separated,
here together only for a short time
by accident, the trees looming
over us as a warning of how
temporary everything is,
that we'll decompose
just like the apple core
we toss into the stream,
that even if we try
we won't last.

Same Frequency

In Monterey, we swap stories from our senior proms.
I tell about my friend giving the DJ a mix CD
featuring "Keasbey Nights," and all the kids
who stayed until the end formed a circular
skank pit and danced.

You're familiar with ska, but not skanking,
so the next morning I demonstrate
in my hotel room, kicking my feet and swinging
my arms. You're entertained, but say you hate
that it's called *skanking.*

You sit in the desk chair, never
moving closer, though I want you to.
My friends have always told me I'm too
innocent, and maybe your hesitation
puts me in good company.

A couple days later,
driving through Soledad and sienna mountains,
"Rude" by Magic! plays in static bursts
on the one radio station we can find
not broadcasting church sermons on Sunday.

It's catchy. I sing along.
You say you hate the lyrics,
that the fictional character in the song
is the rude one, marrying his girl anyway
after her dad says *no.*

I pause before twisting the radio dial.
I used to be attracted to guys
who liked the same music as me,
but now I'm noticing all the more important
layers, appearing in static bursts

like one-second clips of familiar songs
I'd almost forgotten the words to,
while scrolling through the FM band.

WYKYK

I know when I sing along to Matt Maeson in the car
with you next to me and I don't hold back,
don't use my "shy" singing voice.

I know when you rant about how Seth Rogen
is raffling off time to talk ceramics and smoke weed
with him, how you'd apply if it were just ceramics talk.

I know when you talk about your dream of one day
building your own house and your face lights up
when we drive by a house we both like.

I know when I equate organized religion to cults—
an opinion I typically keep to myself—
and you agree without question.

I know when we talk of our shared dreams
to one day make a living off our art:
your ceramics, my writing.

I know when you say you "don't need a kid"
and I sigh in relief after years of pressure
from an ex and his family to have children

I could never see myself happily raising.
How I wish to date someone without the pretense
of a family, of stereotypical American Dreams.

I know now what my therapist meant when
she said I needed to share values with someone.
But I don't know how to make you understand all of this.

In Which I Think We Can Read Each Other's Minds

At the Steinbeck house, you ask to see John's ring,
and when the volunteer goes upstairs to retrieve it
you turn to me and say, "if you don't ask, it will never happen,"
and I feel like that has a double meaning.

Later, at lunch, you tell your mom over the phone
that your one regret was not holding your hand
up to your face for a photo while you wore the ring,
and I don't want to have any regrets on this trip.

Perception

"You need to give me some warning next time
so I don't laugh," I say as we exit the elevator,
but you tell me I'll catch on with practice.
I wonder if you do this with all the girls
you hang out with: wait for a stranger
to enter then look me in the eyes,
slick your hair back, and start on a story
about how grandma called and they'll have
to amputate. Your lips and tone are even.
You've rehearsed this. I was never good
at improv but I try to play along
because I don't want you to think
I'm not fun and spontaneous.

The receptionist at the next hotel
doesn't know what to do with us
after placing two water bottles
on the counter and you telling him,
"she keeps telling me I need to hydrate more."
He looks at us one at a time, stern-faced,
and says, "I know better than to get involved,"
as though we're an old married couple
and not a couple of thirty-somethings
with reservations in separate rooms
because when we booked this trip
you had a girlfriend and we had
a budget to fill.

Two days later, at lunch,
our server apologizes for the wait,
then says, "Though it looks like
you're enjoying each other's company,"
and you say, "we are," before sipping
your iced tea, and I know she knows
there is something lingering under the surface.

Just like the rental car associate
who asked if we were married but gave us
the same rate anyway.
Just like the hiker at Pinnacles
who offered to take our picture and said,
"gorgeous" after each shot.

You're surprised when I tell you I have feelings.
You say you don't often think about
how other people perceive you or the things
you say, but when I ask if you noticed vibes,
you say we have a "connection,"
as if the two can't be synonymous,
as if it isn't obvious to everyone
except you.

Dream Life

Let's open an art studio,
where you'll teach ceramics
and I'll teach creative writing
and we can hold poetry readings
and serve iced tea and hot chocolate.

Let's travel to Acadia,
since you've never been to Maine,
and as we hike Beehive and Cadillac
you can make jokes about how "uphill
and downhill Chelsea are not the same."

Let's build a house
with a view and paint it black.
You can have a flat roof if I can have
a wraparound porch and library, and
there we'll brainstorm our next projects.

But you say you're too old
for such adventures, and you've never
considered dating someone so far from home.
So I guess I'll keep chipping away
at these wild dreams on my own.

Standards

I'm 19, and one of two
straight edge kids at a friend's
twenty-first birthday party.
While everyone else drinks,
the other straight edge kid invites
me across the hall to her dorm.
She brings a guy she wants
to set me up with, tells me
he plays drums and likes math rock.
Apparently my type is predictable.
We hang out and chat about music
and brainstorm corny band names
while *Muppets in Space* plays
in the background.
When he leaves, he tells me
I have the most beautiful eyes
and he hopes he meets me a million
more times. When my friend asks
what I think of him, I say,
"he's cute but I'm not into guys
who do drugs," and she nods and
confirms he does a lot of drugs.
I never see him again.

I'm 34, and freshly out of an
almost decade-long relationship,
finally acknowledging
I couldn't love him fully.
Maybe it was the beer, the whiskey,
the empty cigarette cartons hidden
in junk drawers and the garage.
I spend a week in California with
a guy I met the previous summer
who rants about how alcohol-obsessed
our society is and says he never did
drugs because he didn't see the point.
He is everything I have wanted for years.

We spend our trip hiking and driving
along the Pacific coast, through the mountains,
talking about our friends and families
and lives and with every mile I am more sure
this is the person I am meant to be with.
When I tell him how I feel,
he confesses he has never considered
anything romantic between us,
has to figure out a lot of things about himself,
and now I don't know if I'll ever see him again.

I look around at my friends in relationships,
marriages, and wonder how many
are happy, equally in love.
I create "what if" scenarios in my head,
think about the math rock drummer
and if I had not had such high standards,
if we had seen each other again,
would I now be in this predicament?

My Mother Reads My Tarot Cards

and pulls The Lovers for the umpteenth time.
She tells me I should ask a different question—
we haven't talked in a while and the cards
have brought us together—but really I just want
to know if I'm crazy to trust my gut and see
where things go with the faraway guy.
        We text all the time, and sometimes
        the texts seem flirty, but it's hard to tell.

She pulls the Knight of Cups and asks
if I'm on birth control, confirms there are
mutual feelings. Her intuition is spot on
with everyone else and I want to trust
she has the same clairvoyance with me.
        On the first night I see him again,
        he tells me he is recently single
        and it's too uncanny to be coincidence.

When she flips over the Seven of Swords,
she warns of trickery, another person
waiting in the shadows to swoop
one of us away from the other.
        He says he and the girl are transitioning
        to being friends. They Snapchat each other
        when we take breaks from sightseeing
        and I know his heart is elsewhere.

After the trip, after a tense goodbye
that leaves me sobbing in the airport,
I ask what will come of us. My mom turns over
the Ten of Cups—happy family—and I'm not sure
if she's reading my love life or our own
renewed bond. I wonder if this is all
an exercise in patience, in timing, or whether
her tarot powers work on everyone except me.

Robot Poem

On the Pacific Coast Highway, you read a list from your phone of things you've said that other people describe as "robot phrases." I think they're funny

until we say goodbye at the airport and you refuse a hug and offer a handshake instead. "I don't want to give mixed signals," you say, as if the damage isn't already done. As if the man standing in front of me is not the one I just traveled with for nine days.

Instead of responding to your "made it home safely" text, I hike Griffith Park in ninety-degree heat and eat rolled ice cream in Koreatown and try to make sense of this parting. My cousins— both actors, both optimists—reassure me over brunch that there will be another chapter.

I don't want to force anything and I don't want you to ghost me. I just want us to be able to talk again like we used to, without getting texts with less emotion than ChatGPT

so I sit and count the weeks,
                    then months,

since I interacted with a living, breathing you,
hoping California wasn't the last time.

The Voice in My Head

My ex always told me I had ADHD,
that I was inconsiderate

because I'd space out during conversations
because I'd seem like I didn't care

but really I was having a conversation
with the voice in my head.

It's always been there—
I talk to it while hiking, cleaning, driving,

walking the dog, grading papers.
I tell the voice all about my day,

about stories from when I was growing up,
the stories I'm writing,

the adventures I'd like to go on with
this fictional voice if they were real.

When we're in California,
I find myself telling these same stories

with the same energy and passion
and when you tell stories of your own

you have my complete attention.
I do not hear a separate voice in my head.

But when I return home
I'm met with a silence I've never experienced.

No one to tell about my day,
via text or just in my head,

and I've never felt so alone.

Release

They say trauma is stored in the hips.
Maybe this was my flaw in past relationships
but now I feel it in my entire body
when I lie in savasana—
how my limbs start to shake
and I break down crying uncontrollably, for hours,
even when I've gone the whole day
without forming your name
on my lips.

The Next Time Someone Tells Me to Get Over It

I really might just quit my job,
sell my house, and buy a cabin
in the middle of the woods
where I'll write books about
how much more sense life
would make if we were together.

The next time someone says,
"You can do better," I'll ask them
to go out and find it for me
if they think they can feel the weight
of meeting and losing
their dream person.

I'll ask them to explain to the next
potential suitor that I want my legacy
to be my art, not small humans who will
maybe look like me, that I spent too many
years not knowing how to love my body
and I'm not giving up control of it now.

I'll ask them to explain that it's not
that I don't like being touched,
but the smell of alcohol and cigarettes
makes me want to vomit.
So no, I don't want to kiss a man
who does these things,

and no, I don't care if he says,
"but I'm not an alcoholic."
Because they'll need to explain
how it transports me back
to a kid waiting for her mom
to come home from the bar.

Because "you're bound to date someone
like your parents" sounds like
perpetuating generational trauma
and I'm done with that shit.
Because I've already met someone
who meets my standards,

and anyone else just won't add up,
because anyone else will read
these poems and know they can't
compete, because I want a good story
and I want it to end happily.
I'm not just looking for a muse.

Because I'm not just some naive girl
who doesn't know what love is.
I know everyone has flaws.
I just want us to have a chance,
and I don't think that's asking
for too much.

222

You say astrology and tarot are fake
but you've made an angel number part of your personality.

You say the number is just a Kanye reference
yet you etch it in clay and print it on jerseys.

You tell me the story of the time you ordered
two thousand dollars' worth of two-dollar bills

from the bank, how you leave them with tips
at restaurants and elsewhere to make people smile.

You rank sightings of 222 in the wild on a scale of 1-5.
It's endearing. So I send you pictures of:

> A tire cover with a tiger face above a 222: 4.0
> My car in parking spot 222 at the train station: 4.2
> An incorrect phone number, all 2's, on a pizza
> receipt: 4.8

You say this is just a silly thing you do,
but I know it's deeper than that.

222 miles separate the towns we each grew up in.
And months after we've last spoken, I'm still seeing 222s
everywhere:

on necklaces, tattoos, while scrolling or playing cards,
and I want to believe the universe is keeping us connected.

Spring Again

This time last year,
I would lie awake at 3am
typing notes on my phone
of how I would reveal
my feelings to you.
This year I want to feel
anticipation for something—
for you—I could feel that
changes were approaching
the spring before we met,
but now everything is so uncertain.

My school needs a new
ultimate frisbee coach
and I consider applying
but something holds me back.
It's your sport, and
I'm worried it will make me
too hopeful that we'll talk again,
that I'll text to discuss strategy,
and I'm afraid that if I don't
do it, I'll never feel close
to you again like I did
at camp and California
and all the time in between.

I coach track instead,
but during practice
I find myself gazing out
onto the ultimate field,
watching the disc glide
over the 50-yard line
like a drone capturing a scene
in an alternate life:

one where you are on the sidelines
wearing a youthful grin
as you relish sharing your passion
with the students. And I know
it can be different,
that you can be here right now,
and after practice ends we can return
to the same home and talk
about our days and dreams
and be each other's biggest
cheerleaders.

And it might sound crazy,
so different from how we pictured
our lives, but think about it:
how many lives we've already lived,
how many more lives are still
in our futures.
And though some days
it feels pointless, the only thing
that makes sense is that someday,
some of those lives
we can experience together.

With Thanks

First and foremost, thank you to the members of my writers group—Lisa McKay, Natalie Schriefer, Deb Silber, and Shelley Stoehr—for recognizing I had a chapbook in the works before I fully knew what I was writing. Thank you to mychael zulauf for your encouraging words about my poems and motivating me to actually complete the chapbook. Thanks to Mark and Nicole Bouchard for helping me figure out which early drafts went together, and Emilia Caturano for your feedback once I had a full manuscript. Thank you to Joanna Douglas for being my "Instagram boyfriend" and capturing the perfect author photo. A big thank you to Victoria Buitron for your close attention to detail and some late-stage suggestions that helped the book out a lot. More poetry picnics, please. And finally, thank you to A, without whom these poems would not exist. I will always remember our California trip fondly.

Chelsea Dodds is a writer and teacher from Connecticut. She holds an MFA from Southern Connecticut State University, and her writing has been published in *The Forge, Maudlin House, Rejection Letters, Poetry Super Highway, Sixfold Journal,* and the *2024 Connecticut Literary Anthology* (Woodhall Press). When not writing, Chelsea can usually be found hiking, practicing yoga, or planning her next road trip. You can read more of her work at *chelseadodds.com.*

www.ingramcontent.com/pod-product-compliance
Lightning Source LLC
Chambersburg PA
CBHW022044080426
42734CB00009B/1232